HOW TO SHOW A SENIOR CITIZEN YOU LOVE THEM

12 EASY IDEAS YOU CAN DO ANYTIME

I0106564

Stephanie Weiger

Stephanie Weiger
stephanie.weiger@gmail.com

Ordering Information:
Quantity sales. Special discounts are available on quantity purchases by corporations, associations, and others. For details, contact the author at the address above.

How to Love a Senior Citizen/ Stephanie Weiger. —1st ed.
ISBN 979-8-9871523-0-0

Dedicated to my family

CONTENTS

Introduction

Growing up, my grandparents were my only babysitters. They would spend the evening, putting my brother and me to bed when our parents were out to dinner. I didn't grow up geographically near cousins on my mom's side and my dad was an only child.

My brother and I were often the only kids at holiday functions and family dinners. We spent most of our time with older relatives.

Spending my youth primarily around older people, obviously had an effect on me. During my master's degree in social gerontology, I secured an internship in an assisted living facility while also working in a nursing home.

For the last 25 years I have spent my time building relationships, having fun and loving senior citizens. The covid pandemic shined a light on the need to regularly connect with older loved ones. I hope this book provides a few tips, ideas and inspiration for you, that showing a senior citizen you love them can be fun and easy to do!

CHAPTER ONE

Call

Call your senior citizen on the phone or via video chat. If your loved one lives in an apartment building with an activities department, because of the recent covid pandemic, the staff may be more equipped to facilitate a video call for you.

Keep in mind:

*Speak slowly

*Speak loudly, but don't yell or scream

*Avoid computer or technical terms or slang that may confuse your senior or make them feel left out of the conversation

*Have the grandkids or young family members make the phone call - it's good practice for kids to use the phone and they will have a kind, loving and interested audience to hear their stories

*If children are contacting your senior citizen, practice what they will say or ask, ahead of time - write ideas on notecards as reminders

*If making a video call, have someone with a steady hand hold the recording device so your loved one can see who is talking or what is happening clearly

*Schedule a different family member to call your loved one on a rotating schedule

*Make a large print, custom phone book so your senior can contact family members anytime

CHAPTER TWO

Speak Clearly

With advanced age, some senior citizens experience hearing and vision challenges. It can take longer to process conversation, and reply, especially if they can't see you well, and if there is background noise or multiple people in the room.

Keep in Mind:

*Be prepared to repeat what you say, if your senior doesn't hear you the first time, or it doesn't make sense to them

*If it's safe to have an in-person visit with your senior citizen, ask to turn off the TV or loud music during your visit

*If you are able to let them see your face as you talk, it can make communication and understanding easier

*Choose a space that is quiet and where all of you can focus on your time spent together

*Remind children ahead of the visit, to look at the elderly loved one when they are speaking and to enunciate as clearly as possible

*Prepare everyone in advance if there has been a health change for your senior

*Avoid using slang or pop culture terms that may be unfamiliar to senior citizens, so everyone feels included in the conversation

CHAPTER THREE

Send flowers

Everyone loves getting flowers and you don't have to send them just on major holidays. Any day is a good day to get flowers!

Keep in mind:

*If you live close, you can pick flowers up at the grocery store and deliver them yourself

*If you have small children in your family, they can pick flowers and bring them in a jelly jar or paper cup

*If you don't live nearby, but know someone who does, ask them to get flowers for your loved one and drop them off – you can reimburse them electronically

*Check online coupon sites for deals on flower delivery

*Choose a live plant that will last longer than cut flowers in order to remind your senior citizen of you each time they see it and care for it, if they are able to do so

CHAPTER FOUR

Write a note

Everyone likes to get notes, cards or letters in the mail. This is an easy day-brightener for everyone: for you when you send it, and for your elderly loved one when they receive it!

Keep in mind:

*You don't have to use a special card - plain copy paper is fine

*Your note doesn't have to be long - use a blank note card or even a postcard from your town or somewhere you've visited to let your senior know you are thinking of them

*Consider starting an intergenerational pen pal correspondence with younger family members and your senior citizen

*If your loved one has vision challenges, using a black permanent marker and writing in big block print may help them read your message independently

*Put your senior's birthday or other special days on your calendar and send some handwritten love before those dates so your note arrives on time

CHAPTER FIVE

Send photos

There are a lot of easy photo sharing and printing options available. You can even print photos at home. Senior citizens may not use digital technology or have an electronic device, but that doesn't mean you can't share photos with them.

Keep in Mind:

*Edit the photos so that the main subject is more easily seen in the printed version - zoom in on faces or eliminate confusing backgrounds

*If your elderly loved one has vision challenges, consider ordering 5x7 or larger pictures - find coupon codes online to make this option more economical

*Label pictures on the back, with family member's names if your senior citizen has memory loss or confusion

*Try a photo delivery service to make sending photos even easier

CHAPTER SIX

Send artwork

Sending any kind of art is a fun way to connect. Sharing kids' school projects with elderly loved ones is a great way to keep in touch and keep them in the loop about what the kids are doing in school.

Keep in Mind:

*Coloring pages, for kids or adults, are an easy way to send artwork to your loved one, and there are countless options

*If you or your siblings paint or draw - consider sending art created by adults, as well as art made by kids

*Include tape or refrigerator magnets for easy display options

*Purchase a special snap frame for your senior citizen to make it easier to update and put new art on display

*If you are not artsy, support local artists when you visit art fairs, craft shows or boutiques, and share an artist's unique creative endeavors with your loved one while supporting an entrepreneur

CHAPTER SEVEN

Send a care package

Care packages aren't just for college students. Senior citizens enjoy being remembered with treats in the mail too.

Keep in Mind:

*For an easy care package, brainstorm items that will fit in an envelope that your senior citizen would enjoy - a poem, a special bookmark, a joke or riddle, a chocolate bar, origami, socks, a tea bag, a favorite recipe, stamps, some trivia or fun facts

*For a bigger care package, think about what kinds of snacks or treats your senior citizen has enjoyed over their lifetime - can you find an old fashioned cookie brand or favorite flavor of theirs

*If they enjoy crossword puzzles or word finds, there are large print versions available for those with vision impairment

*Consider if your senior would like to listen to audio books in the winter or work on a colorful jigsaw puzzle

*Maybe your loved one would enjoy a small teddy bear or stuffed animal to hold

*Care packages are a great idea on special holidays as well - and you can include items

that match the theme such as green accessories to wear for St. Patrick's Day, or a heart decoration to hang on their door for Valentine's Day

*Don't forget to send a note explaining the items you chose to send in the care package

CHAPTER EIGHT

Ask Questions

Simply asking your senior citizen thoughtful questions about their life can unleash so much information about them and their family, and give you a more detailed glimpse of their lived history.

Keep in Mind:

*Brainstorm what questions you want to ask them before your visit or call

*Consider topics based on what's happening in your own family life at the time or current world events

*Have children or young family members interview your senior citizen for an intergenerational activity and perspective

*If you are having a hard time coming up with questions to ask, research conversation starter ideas online

*Assign someone to be the conversation recorder - either on paper or digitally, so that you can enjoy the stories and information they share for years to come

*Sign up your senior citizen for a story sharing subscription where they can record their stories in a book format

*Be considerate of topics your senior may not want to talk about, such as the death of a loved one or their military service

CHAPTER NINE

Bring a treat

If you have a busy schedule, but can visit on your way home from work, or on a weekend afternoon, bring a special dessert or easy appetizers like cheese and crackers, to enjoy with your loved one.

Keep in Mind:

*Let them know you are coming so they can put on a pot of coffee or tea, and get out appropriate dishes

*Let your senior know ahead of time how long you can stay

*You don't have to make a homemade dessert - store bought treats are yummy and the time you spend together will be very appreciated

*Make it a regular or weekly event, if possible

*If you have more time, consider making their favorite cookie or cake recipe with them when you visit

*Bring to-go containers so they can share some of their dessert with their neighbors or friends, or so you can take home a sample of the baked goods you made together

CHAPTER TEN

Pick Up Groceries

Everyone needs to eat. Shopping can be a challenge for senior citizens due to lack of trasnportation or mobility issues. If your senior cooks their own food, grocery shopping for them is a thoughtful way to show them love (since you have to do your own shopping anyway).

Keep in Mind:

*Grocery shopping for senior citizens at a local store is a great task for newly minted teen drivers to do

*If your senior citizen lives on their own, the gift of an online grocery delivery order is another way to shop for them

*Remember elderly neighbors who may be homebound

*Bring all the ingredients for their favorite dish or an easy recipe that comes together using shelf stable goods - they can make it for a future meal

*If your senior citizen is no longer able to cook for themselves, consider a midday meal delivery service as a gift for them

*Even if your loved one no longer cooks, and has meals provided for them in their senior living community, everyone has a favorite snack or beverage they've enjoyed over their lifetime - add it to your grocery list and deliver or send it to your senior

CHAPTER ELEVEN

Visit

If you live close by, and it's safe to do so, an in-person visit is a great way to show your senior citizen some love.

Keep in Mind:

*<u>Put your phone or digital device away</u>

*<u>Have your kids and family members put their digital device away too</u>

*Think about your goal and timeframe for the visit before you go, and share that plan with your family members or friends who will be joining you

*If you want to show photos, print them out ahead of time and write names and dates on the back so your loved one can reflect on the people and stories in the pictures, after your visit

*Prep children or young visitors about speaking loud enough so your senior citizen can hear them, and what topics they might want to share about themselves

*Prior to your visit, explain to young children, why your senior is now using an assistive device such as a walker or hearing aid, and give the kids recommendations for the best way to interact

*Brainstorm some questions to ask your loved one about their recent activities

*Bring an easy-to-play card game for everyone to enjoy

*Bring a dog or other pet to join the visit

*If you have small children accompanying you, bring along a soft ball or balloon so everyone can play catch

*Bring a snack or special treat for everyone to enjoy

*Ask if you can do a task for your senior citizen - consider mentioning this to them before your visit in case you need to bring special tools or items to complete the task

*If your senior has limited mobility, take them for a short walk or a ride in their wheelchair during your visit, in order for them to get a change of scenery or see a different part of their building or neighborhood

CHAPTER TWELVE

Visiting in Memory Care

If your loved one is living in a nursing home or memory care setting, here are a few extra ideas to keep in mind when sending them love through the mail or when you visit in person.

Keep in Mind:

*Because names and faces can get lost with age or dementia, when sending a card, include a picture of who the card is from (you), so that your senior can more easily recognize the sender

*If your senior citizen has trouble chewing or swallowing, do not send hard candy or nuts because these items can be choking hazards - consider something softer like pudding, soft cookies or cupcakes instead

*For in-person visits, put away your cell phone and focus on your senior citizen - set this expectation with young people who are also visiting with you

*Your loved one may not remember who you are, your name, or how you are related - avoid quizzing them as this is stressful and embarrassing if they cannot remember the answers - they **will** remember how you made them feel, so make them feel happy and loved

*Your senior citizen may not understand what you are saying or asking them - if they have dementia, their brain is not working the same way it used to work, but they most likely enjoy seeing you and being with you during the visit (depending on their mood)

*Some days are harder than others for people with dementia and if the visit isn't going well or they seem upset, it might be wise to try again another day

*Be patient - if your loved one has hearing loss and dementia, it will take much longer for them to understand what you said

*Your senior may not be able to find the correct word when they are speaking – remember to be patient and kind and read their facial expressions for more clues

*It may be easier on them, and for you, to plan for more frequent, but shorter visits

*When possible, avoid visiting at meal times - if that's your only option, be prepared to sit with your loved one while they eat, or even

assist them with their meal while you visit with everyone at their table

*If your senior citizen is getting anxious or upset, try a simple distraction, such as going for a walk down the hall, or a roll in their wheelchair to an outside patio - a change of scenery can do a lot to shift the mood of someone with dementia

*Plan to share a sensory experience with your loved one during your visit - listening to favorite music or singing, doing some sort of movement, holding hands, rubbing their back, combing their hair, petting a dog, washing their hands with them, painting their fingernails, tasting cookies you made, smelling newly mown grass or favorite flowers

*Have low expectations when you visit your senior citizen in a nursing home or memory care - having lofty goals that they will recognize you, that you will have a riveting conversation, or that it will be a festive experience, may set you and your family up for disappointment and create hesitation about future visits

*Remember the goal of your visit is to share love with your senior, where they are in their life journey and let them know you care about them in a way they can enjoy

FINAL THOUGHTS

The ideas outlined in this book are just the beginning of what you can do to show love to a senior citizen. The possibilities are endless. Knowing your senior's abilities and interests will open up many opportunities to show them love. If you are still at a loss as to what your senior citizen might enjoy, it's as easy as picking up the phone and asking them how you can connect. The time you spend together and the memories made, will be priceless.

ABOUT THE AUTHOR

Stephanie Weiger is a social gerontologist. She has worked in senior living communities for 25 years and is currently part of a super fun activities staff. She has lived her whole life in Minnesota. Stephanie loves brainstorming ideas, planning events, and has called hundreds, maybe thousands of games of bingo. This is her first book, though probably not the last. She can be reached at stephanie.weiger@gmail.com.